ANCHOR BOOKS

POLITICALLY CORRECT

Edited by

Suzy Goodall

First published in Great Britain in 1997 by
ANCHOR BOOKS
1-2 Wainman Road, Woodston,
Peterborough, PE2 7BU

HB ISBN 1 85930 427 3
SB ISBN 1 85930 422 2

Foreword

Anchor Books is a small press, established in 1992, with the aim of promoting readable poetry to as wide an audience as possible.

We hope to establish an outlet for writers of poetry who may have struggled to see their work in print.

The poems presented here have been selected from many entries. Editing proved to be a difficult and daunting task and as the Editor, the final selection was mine.

We are continually hearing the views of politicians regarding what they can do for you, but what do you - the people that count - really think?

Over 100 poets have come together to voice their opinions on many of the key issues such as school funding, the NHS and homelessness.

This anthology has given the authors a chance to express their thoughts and feelings to today's top people.

I trust this selection will delight and please the authors and all those who enjoy reading poetry.

Suzy Goodall
Editor

CONTENTS

WHO CARES WHAT THE NEWSPAPERS SAY?

The crime rate has never been higher,
House values continue to fall,
We're not coming out of recession,
It seems there's no future at all.

But we shouldn't give way to pure panic,
Who cares what the newspapers say?
They try to get more and more readers
With sensational headlines each day.

The end of the world is upon us!
A virus will wipe out mankind!
The monarchy's started to crumble!
If you eat the wrong food you'll go blind!

When you look at the horoscope column
And it forecasts disaster for you,
Turn over the page and ignore it -
Predictions don't always come true!

Gladys Law

THE DREAMING

I dream Armageddon,
Mutually assured destruction.
Hands of a crazy man poised,
Life and death at his command.

I dream famine,
Pitiful cries from a starving child.
The stench of the dying,
The West in shame, opulent, overfed.

I dream nights of madness,
The Idd monsters abroad.
Casting their spells, feeding on fear,
Haunting my mind.

I dream a thousand images,
Dreams of the past.
An ever changing future,
They come, tormenting, enticing.

I dream black and white,
Pastels and greys.
A twisting kaleidoscope of colours,
Shines through, the psychedelic haze.

I dream Utopia,
Man's prejudice tamed.
A world of harmony,
Love, and understanding.

David Pocock

THE TIME THE PLACE

With celebrity swagger he announces the theme
Sincere raised eyebrows beneath greying hair
From 'Abortion' to 'A Midsummer Night's Dream'
Let us all revel in television despair
Look deep into the camera Eileen
Relive for us the death of your son, thirteen.

Tell us exactly how did you feel
And I'll cock my head with feigned interest.
After he died, did you pray? Did you kneel?
The tears on camera 3 look best
Share with the world your hex appeal
And regarding the re-runs, we'll cut you a deal

Sell your soul for the ratings' sake
Yes open your mouth, your hearts and brain
Let us listen to the crack as your heart breaks.
We didn't catch that sob, could you do it again?
Cry real tears, love, we don't want fake
And can you try and finish before the commercial break?

Tell us about the wife you've lost Mr Lear
Do you miss her at night when you're all alone?
Do you beat up your kids? Do you drink too much beer?
Do you wake up crying 'cos you're on your own?
With my jaw clenched manly. I'll lean forward in my chair
And ask your kids if they miss their mother dear.

I'll paint a picture of sadness on a canvas bleak
A TV square of sour knowledge dawning
I'll anger the angered and pity the meek
In half hourly spots every weekday morning
Yes Kilroy was here with subsidised grace
The rhyme, the crime, the time, the place.

Darren Stapleton

MY VOICE

I see too much within the world, I feel its pain too keenly.
I've seen and understood too much about those that are my people
And my voice makes little difference in a society that worships money.
I hate my race for what it has done and pity it for what it has become,
For within its self-obsession it is oblivious to what it is doing.

I want to feel the rainfall and not worry about acid rain.
I want to tell my children that it's safe for them today to play.
I want to be able to walk where I please without my can of Mace.
I want to know that wildlife is not used or killed but lives and grows.
I want to see the forests grow and stretch across the world.
I want to see the killing and hunger end, for there is no need for it.
I want the impossible from a cold uncaring race.

Our reign cannot last forever, everything must come to an end.
What will our explanation be when we are brought to book for our crimes.
Sorry about the deforestation? The murder and the mutilation.
We did not really mean to create the hole in the sky.
Our legends tell us of people who understood what we do not.
They kept the balance, they did not let greed and ignorance rule them.
I see a race that is hell bent on self-destruction, a race at war with itself.
Prove me wrong, give me the world that I desire, give me hope for I am your
future.

Julie Lynne Rickett

CAN WE COUNT ON YOU, SIR?

When the elections were held in our town
They came to each door in our street.
'We're the party that cares for the people,
With promises for those we meet.

Now we want to improve your conditions.
We want you to know that we care.
Your street lighting is due for improvement.
The potholes we'll fill in right there.

Those large trees are soon due for pruning.
The shopping arcade will be new.
We'll put benches quite near to the bus-stop
A crossing quite close to it too.

Yes, the park is now rather an eyesore
And not very safe late at night.
Well we've plans to landscape it completely.
Please trust us and we'll get it right.'

Now they seemed so sincere and straight-forward.
They saw I was keen and took note.
'Can we ask you whom you are supporting?'
I said 'You can count on my vote!'

They got in! They now run the council.
I'm just as fed up as before.
Lighting and potholes are still just as bad.
The trees have spread out even more.

The shopping parade now cancelled for good.
The benches no longer a need.
They've said the crossing is not now required
Whilst the park has just gone to seed.

'Vote for us' they said. 'Things will be different.
We're the party of action!' they said.
I know the action I'm taking next time.
I'm voting to stay home in bed!

John Christopher Cole

THE CHAIRMAN

At the meeting he sat there in silence,
An onlooker at the affray.
They forgot he was there, sitting slumped in his chair,
While the rest fought to get in their say.
The zealots put forward ideals,
The lawyers mapped pitfalls and mines,
The idle said go for the old status quo.
The ambitious just tangled the lines.
The whizz-kids went off at a tangent,
The timid were backing the field,
The Company Men looked for precedents, then
The accountants complained of the yield:
And he sat there and listened in silence
'Til he'd heard all the arguments through
Then he put to each one what he thought should be done:
Which is what they decided to do.

Tim Norfolk

LABOUR OF LOVE

When conservative policies are mentioned
My mood arrives at fever pitch,
It seems to me
The only ones who benefit from them,
Are the rich.

I've just two words for John,
(The *major* obstacle
In the conservative party)
Be gone!

I've always supported Labour
For they,
Like Robin Hood,
Look out for the poor,
The middle and working class,
Levelling out the riches from the greedy
To the old and needy,
Giving a fair share for all,
And surely that can only be good.

So come on folks!
Don't pass,
Let's be fair,
When next it's time to vote
Don't abstain
And say you don't care,
Put on your coat,
And mark your cross next to the one who represents
Labour and Tony Blair.

Molly Wrigley

VOTE FOR THE CANNABIS PARTY

Last summer the Lib Dems
At their Brighton AGM
Voted 426 to 375
To keep our campaign alive

Not long ago between world wars
A bad decision walked the boards
And cannabis or hemp illegal became
Since then medicine from alcohol gained?

And pornography blossomed
The arms trade too
It's only cannabis can't get to you!
The politics of this
None comprehend
Only doctors don't
Die in the end?
Alcohol it seems is king
And spatted ciggys
Pretty things.
The Cannabis Party
Needs your vote
Legalise it
Please don't gloat!
The Labour Party's fudging it
The Conservative Party too
Free all those police resources
Re-legalise it
That's what you should do.
Vote for the Cannabis party,
Free Tibet, Mordechai Vanunu, and stop big Hinkley C.
Thank you.

Jesu Ah'so

THE PERSUADERS

It's that time of year again,
What an awful bore,
When those smart men in suits and ties,
Come knocking at my door,
I peer around my curtain wondering who it could possibly be,
Yet another salesman or maybe the vicar joining me for tea,
I wait patiently as they switch on their false bright faces and
twiddle their rosettes,

They ask politely if they can have my vote,
I politely answer I haven't decided yet,
They seem to have forgotten the simple things, these ladder
climbing men,
For I have seen and heard more than they will ever learn,
They tell me things they think I ought to know then thrust their
leaflets in my hand,
And as I close the door I remember friends I lost, protecting
this green and pleasant land,
We were all important then as we proudly marched so brave
and fine,
But now it seems we are only important around election time.

B A Hynds

SILENT DISARRAY

A prisoner of war, in my own mind,
I will take you on an adventure, in the caverns of my soul,
Where the tongueless madman, expresses his feelings,
Through barbed wire charisma,
Penned in his home of silent disarray,
Come to me today, no toll gates to pay, the fee of insanity.

A child swings on his highchair,
Nearer to his destiny and moral decay,
A rapist rapes, a woman cries, a vicar dies,
A fish's gills, fill with oil,
A rainforest seed, no one to heed,
Is washed away, in the death machine's greed,
Angels cry, but why, but why,
Fleeing the blood stained sunset, which caresses the sky.

Mark Underwood

LEADERS: HEAVEN HELP US!

Thatcherism's gone and left the day
A Government that's useless for today
No good leader, disastrous now to all
For they try in vain to reign and rule.

Privatisation's everything then and now
The Government's nought but a useless stupid cow
All thoughts are gone of hope and needs and care
Nought in its place but poverty and despair.

And what hope for the future may one ask
We really ought to take the sods to task
But all the while they get filthy rich
The poor one is regarded as the bitch.

Mary Hayworth

ECONOMIC RECOVERY

Hands round your faithful pint:
The man in the blue rosette is lying on TV
And the beggars are singing 'Happy days are here again'

The Job centre: a mad cow in a blue
Rosette says how lucky you are
To be free of your job

Queue for work: one fifty an hour.
Millionaire in the blue rosette asks
If you're proud
To help his tax cut

Eight PM: a cold clear night
Transvestite stops a passing car
The driver checks they've got what he wants
The man in the blue rosette buys some crack.

Street cleaner thinks of bed, now filled
By another so the man
In the blue rosette
Can walk on dying men
Who once lived under cardboard

And as they die the man in the blue rosette
Smiles
'Labour's lost another vote'

The green shoots of recovery,
Rooted in mad cow manure,
Come up blue rosettes
And the beggars are singing
'Happy days are here again'

Alex Kashko

CHANGING VOTES

Blue youths imbued with party greed
Maturity marched to idealistic red instead
Green grew gradually into middle age
And beyond -
A fully opened flower
Perfumed with holistic purpose
Planted a cross by rainbow clouds
In natural law and unification
Of humanity in meditation.

Brenda Dove

WHO CARES?

Her bed it is cold, a grey paving stone,
And yesterday's *news* her blanket will be
Huddled in misery, chilled to the bone,
Lost and forgotten, a drop-out she!

An old man sifts through a litter bin
Looking for things others don't care for,
His thin frayed coat held fast by a pin,
He's flotsam washed up on an unfriendly shore.

You'll find them in basements, with little to comfort,
Too tired and depressed to journey abroad,
Fettered by sickness, brought low by discomfort,
Existing is all that they can afford

Who cares for the old, the sick and the poor
The unemployed youth this Government spurns?
Hide them away - forget their existence
Isn't that now this Government's law?

Margaret Sparvell

JOURNA-LISTS

There are journalists and journalists.
Know what I mean?
A film critic writing in the dark comes up to pay
homage to the film star, on the way to the bar.

Every day headlines shriek. Of murder, mayhem we speak.
Haiti - will your journalist last the week?
Money comes from sugar cane, cotton, corruption and cocaine.

Ireland's murder machine is evil and the most obscene.
Trevor McDonald says he was afraid. 'Though we risk it,
Eire takes the biscuit!'

I'd rather not be Kate Adie, that most courageous lady.
Nearer home I might interview a celeb who says
'My marriage wasn't right.
I'll not remarry in all my days.'
He's wed when I go to press and my editor's all stress.
Serves me right
for thinking that I can write the truth - uncouth?

Six o'clock news
shows bloody bodies bruised, of children, the most abused.
Cruelty beyond measure gives Bosnians pleasure,
while I'm tripping over the mat
at the Dorchester
to discuss the beauty of a hat
with the excellent David Shilling.

Peggy Trott

PERSONAL EFFECTS

She looked old, tired, puffy-eyed
As she opened the bag and looked inside.
What did it matter now he was dead?
Some coins, a pen, a screwed-up note,
A tee shirt, slashed and stained with red
From stab wounds to the chest and throat.
The case is closed, the damage done.
This is all that's left of her murdered son.

Angela Lord

FLEET STREET

You have misunderstood me.
I covet neither your title
nor your fancy hat to impress.
I'm a writer
and cannot be more than that,
though I could be,
I could be less.

Thomas Land

EDMUND CLERIHEW BENTLEY OFFERS HIS COMMENTS ON THE GOVERNMENT'S PLANS FOR TOTAL FUNDHOLDING

Virginia Bottomley
Prescribes lobotomy
Knowing it is the ultimate cure
For over-expenditure.

Emily Wills

POLITICS

Politics, I don't really understand them at all!
Like hitting my head against a wall.
So this year I thought, I'd listen to,
Every party's broadcast, to hear their view.

As they spoke, one thing I couldn't digest,
Each party said, they were the best!
All of them said the things they would do,
Each of them promising, 'The best for you!'

So I turned to the papers to read,
The different opinions were hard to concede.
Each paper it seems, has a political flare,
By now, I am nearly pulling out my hair.

In desperation, I switch on the TV,
Watching Parliament, will educate me!
But this only adds to my miserable plight,
For all they seemed to do, was argue and fight.

After all this, I'm no wiser today,
Will my vote change a thing, anyway?
My solution will make the MP's Tut! Tut!
I'll put down my mark, with my eyes firmly shut!

Denise Sanders

IN TRUST

There was a young man named Kinnock
Shouting: Oh! Flipping 'eck.
They're demoralising the nurses
And pinching their purses.
It's the NHS they're trying to wreck!

Nick Colton

SOCIALIST WAKE UP

Whigs and wets
Pains the neck
We total wrecks
Governing techs
Becoming specks
On bloody decks.

Talking Major
He's no saviour
Brixton tutor
More like suitor
Government's Tailor
Bloody traitor.

Tressel's pen
On working men
Forgetting zen
Feeding cozen
Bossy foremen
Bloody frozen.

Socialist drama
Opens Valhalla
With its dogma
Shifting nebula
Labour's dilemma
Bloody umbrella.

Smith's heir
Tony Blair
Let him snare
Who goes where
All compare
Who's bloody chair.

E T Ward

WHAT OF AMBITION?

What of ambition,
is it: greed for money; possessions;
tense craving for power; obsessions
driving a soul to exceptional deeds
and sheer exhaustion?
Or is it: the desire to make life
simple for others; release from strife;
tirelessly aiming for truthfulness and
universal bliss?

Jennifer Travers

IN THE SHOWROOM

Two long rows of televisions
Frame his desperate face
Talking of the ravaged land
He has just left.

Watch his eyes
See how they plead
See how they beg
For understanding.

But there is no sound
To distract the customers
Here only profit screams
And compassion is dumb.

Richard Stewart

ROUGH JUSTICE

I compared, for an experiment,
The wage I get each week
With my total cash, if unemployed,
Now future times look bleak.

If I was on just benefit
My rent would all be paid,
But my income now is just above
The limit: full rent stayed.

No Poll-tax rebate, not at all,
For workers just like me,
But if I was now on the dole
I'd get it paid for free.

And if I didn't work at all
Travel costs wouldn't exist;
That would be one more expense
To be crossed off the list.

One less bill is my catalogue
(Though this may be despondent),
The agent's insurance would pay it off
If I was made redundant.

So how much better off am I,
And what's the final bid?
For working forty hours
I'm better off by eighteen quid!

Cosmic Carrie

POVERTY

'Three kids, and now another on the way.
You look so smug. What does your man say?
No prospects, in a crowded room, with lives so grey.'
'He'll have no opinion. He cares not either way.'

'Spare a muse for that poor little mite.
Coiled, warm and drifting, safe and tight.
'Till bloody, it bursts upon its destiny's blight.
Its mystery gone after the first sight.'

'Let it feed and be nurtured while I can provide that for free.
I will wait for the time when it will love and tend me.'
'You say the child will be a proud branch on the family tree.
I think it will just join you, another victim of poverty.'

'He's out there now, it's not easy it's true,
Looking for paid work to do.
Anyway,
What's it got to do with you?'

'How you must have been neglected of love
To seek it from each kin.
Why can't you realise
You only get out what you put in.'

C Zlotowitz

THOUGHTS OF A REDUNDANT MAN

When the boss called me into the office
I knew my time had come.
I'll have to let you go, he said,
There's not enough work to go round.

Take the money, the boss said,
You'll be alright.
Something will turn up better
For you to make a new start.

I drove home through the traffic
My stomach churning all the way
What could I say to my wife
At the end of a long disillusioning day?

Twenty two years I'd worked there
Long hours and through weekends
Giving up time with my family
Working all hours God sends.

No future, no work, no job,
My dignity and self esteem gone
Join the dole queue just a number
Join the masses but still feel alone.

Gill Sathy

CONSCIENCE

Can you feel their hunger and fear
No comfortable chair no warm bed or beer
How many funds or charity runs
Will it take until the world is one
How precious is life
How much do we care
It's a long way from home
We can't hear their cries they cry alone
What can we do, how can they cope
Brothers and sisters where there's no hope
People loosing limbs and home
Refugees, only life to call their own
Give them some money, write them a cheque
Has it eased your conscience yet
Adopt a baby from 'Tim Buck Two'
It only helps a few
Can you hear a mother cry
When another baby dies
Distribute the wealth and help our friends
Give peace a chance the wars must end

Pam Hornby

MAN'S OWN DESTRUCTION (WHY DON'T THEY LEAVE ME ALONE)?

The world was built a beautiful place,
Until man got silly and gave it a new face.
The deep blue sea, man polluted,
The dark green grass man uprooted.

The dark thick smog that made man cough.
That same thick smog killed the animals off.
Is it all worth it? I ask myself
As I sit back and watch man destroy itself.

Stop this foolishness I often plead
But man has been silly and there's so much greed.
The world that we knew where the birds once sang.
Will suddenly cave in and go with a bang!

Anne-Marie Richardson

LETTER FROM A POOR MAN

Dear Primeminister, Mr John Major,
I am one strong, very poor, black man
I have won, in your oppressive system
despite your attempts
to crush me.
Each time you squeeze,
my energy gets stronger.
Each time you, legislate
your not unracist laws
I gain unseen strength.

But Mr Primeminister, you must remember
we the people, are, but only human.
Watch how much time you spend,
squeezing the poor, poor people.

You may be a major,
but I am no minor.
I am a false Rutherford
and nobody knows
who I really am.

Hey, John Major
don't squeeze the nation,
they might not be crushed.
Instead, Mr Major
they might unite
and crush you instead.

So John Major, Mr Primeminister
don't forget, real power,
is the people of the nation
not yours, Mr primeminister

Semba Jallow-Rutherford

LONDON 1980

Booted girls with chic skim along the pavement.
Middle aged men, monetarism surviving,
Drink complacently, much as they did always.
What are they thinking?

Smartly dressed young men in the trundling tube-train,
Paid inflated salaries making ends meet,
What desires or dreams or despairing torments
Preoccupy them?

Dreams of boats made fast on the Solent? Warm eyes
Teasing with their light that impatient longing?
Laughter, luscious wine, or the din of discos
Drowning their doubting?

Or of balance-sheets, dividends, investments,
Heavy interest rates, running down production?
Do they still fight on in this paper battle,
Guarding the standards

Thrust upon these legions of Mammon's servants
Ruled by hopes of glory and fears of failure,
Set to gain some meritocratic heaven
Lloyd's - underwritten?

Angus Sinclair

H & L OF VAT '94

Home Sweet Home with
             warmth and light,
Has been our nation's true
             delight,
For young and old,
For ill and frail,
In peace and war,
In stress and grief,
A glowing hearth has given
             relief;
But now the dreaded V A T
Will change all that for you
             and me.

The arteries of heat and light
Should not depend on cash
             in hand
But should be everybody's
             right
In this caring, classless land.

Jessica Boak

EEC COUNCIL DIRECTIVE

He can't speak to me anymore,
Reduced to a line on a monitor,
Living off the mains and a drip feed bag.
The jokes about homosexuals and Hitler
are enveloped by a skin graft from his chest,
His cancerous tongue lolling
like a thirsty dog's.
The disinfectant jars
like the cheap lager we used to drink
together.

I hold his hand and make small talk,
Monologues
about the football league tables.
The city skyline glows and flashes now
and someone else will be in our seats
on the top deck.
Chewing their return tickets
and drawing in the condensation on the window.
I'll travel alone tonight
with only an ashtray for company.

EEC Council Directive (89/622/EEC)
says my pocket.

Matthew Humphreys

WHAT PRICE TO PAY?

Society says
'If you're wrong
You must pay!'
How long must it be?
Must it be every day?

Every day of your life
You live in fear
That perhaps not tomorrow
Or even next year . . .

You regret what you've done
You've paid the price right!
Each time that you try
It seems an uphill fight!

So why don't they accept you
Why do you persist?
With pleas for just another chance
That Society resist!

Society run by injustice
Prejudice and bigotry
Making judgements on others
And so the real animals are free!

So when will they stop
And think about you
Forgive and forget
They'll never
That's true!

John McLaren

THE FUTURE

I'm frightened for the future
Will I be ok?
What will happen to my friends,
Upon that fateful day?
The companies will all split up,
And go against each other
With Railtrack watching over them,
The proverbial big brother;
The safety side will disappear,
Slowly bit by bit,
And in its place, some coloured graphs,
Entitled, 'Yearly Profit'
I pray to God I could be wrong,
I hope it doesn't happen
But I really think
That one day soon,
There will be another Clapham.
Oh please bring back the good old days,
Those times I really savour.
I guess that we can get them back,
If we all vote for Labour

G Ellmes

THOSE I HAVE LOATHED

Government cuts stripping services bare
Adults defiling the young in their care
Judges who favour the crook not the victim
Directing sneers at the old bill who nicked him
Uneven, too costly justice; bent cops
Multiples killing off small corner shops
Media loud-mouths . . . the Eltons and Bakers
Currency dealers and quick profit takers

TV brainwashing with placebo soaps
Those who rob youth of its wild dreams and hopes
Vast sums of lottery cash for elitists
Negative equity. National defeatists
Millions on doles when there's work to be done
All thugs who carry a flick knife or gun
Seeing bright minds dulled by doctrinaire teachers
Filth on the media and sewage on beaches

Most politicians. All financial fiddlers.
Privatised share options. Benefit diddlers.
Ruthless drug dealers exploiting the young
Footballers, athletes, demanding a 'bung'
Battery eggs. Wiener Schnitzel. Foie gras.
Drink drivers. Joy riders. Mayhem by car.

So many gripes keep arousing my dudgeon
May be I'm just an old grumbling curmudgeon.

Cyril Mountjoy

THE FOX

The horses they gallop the man and his hounds
The bugle of godless the hooves hit the ground
They're off over hedgerows and fields they do run
To hunt down the fox and kill it for fun?
The fox he is sighted the hounds on the scent
The men on the horses the fox up for rent
The bugle is darkness once more echoes loud
The echo of death the dogs pant and snarl
The hounds have the scent now the fox he must run
The horses they gallop the men having fun
Through hedgerows and fields as miles do pass
The fox he is tired the air he does gasp
Till then in a moment the hounds close the gap
The fox he flows weary he can't beat this trap
The hounds as they circle the fox hits the ground
The pain on the horses the darkness they sound
The order is given the hounds rip the flesh
The fox lays now bleeding as sentenced to death
A man he dismounts calls the hounds now to heal
With the sole of his boot kicks the fox as it squeals
The hunt is then over the fox now lays dead
The huntsmen they stand applaud as they tread
A blood trail leads to a fox in a ditch
A sport so they say a game for the sick
A beautiful creature destroyed for a game
As man the destroyer his footsteps of pain

Lee Robinson

THE DELICATE SAVAGE

Stalking creature with primeval ancestry
Angled body and shining pose.
Black fur spiked with sunlight,
Watching movements darting in daylight,
Is pre-history so far removed?

Birds alert and blackbird signalling.
His cry of alarm in crescendo issuing.
The cat is watchful, always ready.
Stealth personified awaiting fluttering,
Breaking cover and finally trapping.

The hunter crouches, muscles stiffened,
Rippling body flexed for action.
Statuesque in readiness,
To pounce on unwary insects,
And devour in snapping jaw.

Scenting the air and ever listening,
The jungle torment vying with domesticity,
The wild and the homely two in one.
An enigma of man's attachment
With creatures of delicate savagery.

Ann Swandale

WHY, OH WHY

There was a chimpanzee
Full of pain and fear
In its little tiny cage
No-one to shed a tear.

What are they going to do
The doctors with their knives
They'll cut it into pieces
To save some human lives.

Someone will have its heart
Someone will have its liver
It frightens me to death
It really makes me shiver.

Where are all the people
It really makes me think
'Cos if it was a human
They'd be kicking up a stink.

What are those doctors doing
And I often wonder why
Killing these fine creatures
It makes me want to cry.

I'm glad I was a miner
Working down the mine
And not to be a doctor
Just like a Frankenstein.

David Brownley

HARMLESS FUN

It's only sport, just harmless fun.
When the hounds have a fox at bay.
It's far more humane, than to kill with a gun,
Or so the hunters say.
They chase their victim, up hill and down dale,
Through meadows and woodland they'll call,
The prize that they seek is his long bushy tail,
Or his head to hang on a wall.

He's fast and agile, he's cunning and sly,
He's a hunter who abounds while we sleep,
But their horses are faster, and their hounds they will fly,
In pursuit of the quarry they seek.
They say he's a thief, and a villain to boot,
Who I'm sure likes the fun of the chase,
Although that is something he may possibly moot,
As they hound him at a fearful pace.

So why can't they see, it's not harmless fun,
When they chase poor old Reynard around.
There's nothing more barbaric under the sun,
Than to be out with the horse and the hound.
He is only a survivor who means us no harm,
And the hunt is awesomely grim,
But - they will still chase him over hill and small farm,
And rejoice when he's torn limb from limb.

David Galvin

40

THE RESPECT THEY DESERVE

My love for animals
Simple but true
I show them respect
As I would you.

A loving touch
Gentle hand
Defend their honour
I do all I can.

Beaters and bastards
Deserve all they get
Animal cruelty
Makes me upset.

They give us warmth
Without the speech
Abuse their trust
They then become weak.

Put here for a reason
They bring no harm
Cooped up in numbers
Steel framed farms.

Paul Axtell

JUNKIE

Long lank hair pallid face
Of normal emotion there isn't a trace
Sleeve rolled up, hypo there
Another fix, a glassy eyed stare
First it's heroin then cocaine
Injected slowly into a vein
He feels like God just for a while
As on that pallid face appears an inane smile
On Ecstasy he takes a trip
Of many drugs he's in the grip
Death is near he doesn't care
As into space that stony stare
A needle scarred arm a hanging head
He needs another fix he is the living dead

He's hooked.

Peter Lovett

FOOTPRINTS IN MY MIND

Around myself I have a prison wall
Life waits outside, the dreams call,
When the bricks crumble upon my feet
Fear will sound her last heartbeat.

With police holding me in captivity,
The lane of future is of anxiety
No-one can open the door to touch me
The past stole the confidence key.

Holding shattered trust by the window
Those memories unhealed from years ago,
In time when trust sits in my hand
Sight in my eyes will understand.

Jodie L Daniels

EINSTEIN'S INCUBUS (E = MC^2)

he is gone
        his molecules scattered
                at the blink of an eye
                        with the speed of light.

        he saw the flash
his soul blew away
cursing man

                        praying to his God.
                he felt the heat
        his flesh melting
        leaving ghostly shadows

                        future reminders.
                        his family is dust

friends decay
        their village gone

                    from sunburst on the horizon.
                      who pushed the button
                      started the chaos
does it matter?
                civilization is extinct.

                    life extinguished
              at the speed of light
            rubble remains
                where dreams once stood.

W G Denzler

OLD AGE STATE AIDED: THE WORST SCENARIO

Reduced wealth
failed health,
friends dying
time flying,
butt of jokes
by younger folks,
no more adventures
ill fitting dentures,
bodies state aided
beauty faded,
not enough heat
freezing hands and feet,
needing others' kindness
treated as if mindless,
homes sold to meet nursing bills
piles of pills for numerous ills,
the bout of flu you can't shake off
leaving a dry tickling cough,
sounds the death knell
a free bus pass to hell.

Carole Anne Luke

GOD IS THE ANSWER

After many years of heartache,
And many years of pain,
A generation of young folk have grown up,
To know someone who has been killed or maimed.

In this sad and sorry country,
All those murders were in vain,
No matter how long the bereaved will live,
They will always feel the pain.

If only folk, instead would help,
The needy and the ill,
Our country would be a happier place,
When men would cease to kill.

Folk should put their faith in God,
And trust in Him to guide them,
Then a safer place this world would be,
Pray one day soon, that's what we'll see.

For Satan's daily seeking,
His army to increase,
Simply banish him behind you,
And God will give you peace.

Jean Monteith

A HOPE FOR PEACE

I hope the peace is here to stay
Forever and to last
I wish the beatings and the rest
Together now be past
I pray that God will bless our land
And bless our people too
I pray for those who once were hurt
And curse the people who
Will try to put an ending
To this little hope *we* hold
For peace together friendship
Is the way my wish be told
Together living gethering
Together living peace
Together for us one and all
Together trouble cease

Karen Fisher

THE WAY

The young man travelled across Ireland,
Through cities, towns and villages.
He climbed the hills and crossed the valleys
And spoke to the hearts
And minds of men and women,
For He loved Ireland and her people
And longed for their peace.
But they would not listen.
Across the tumult of her dissension
His clear voice called,
'I am the Way
Those who follow Me
Will not walk in darkness -
I am the Christ,
The Son of God,
The Prince of Peace.'

Pearl Reynolds

A BELFAST STORY

In the morning the rain drizzled
dripping from the slates that still remained
to the rafters to the first floor
and through the holes to the kitchen floor below.
The blood had not yet thickened, and diluted in the puddle
but in the dark you wouldn't ever know.
There was no body, and the slogan on the walls
were the same slogans scrawled on other walls around.
There were beer cans and condoms,
disintegrating butts of cigarettes and plastic bags hardened with glue.
These you could see.
The street was empty; all the houses
made an adventure playground for the kids. They play
Provies and UVF. Just like we used to play
Cowboys and Indians. Just as innocent. But of course
no cowboys and no Indians were waiting
in dark doorways to recruit us
with promises of beer and manliness.
By dawn there was no trace of blood.
If someone staggered to a hospital
to have a wound sewn up it didn't reach the news.
The blood was all dispersed. The air
was washed clean of smell. Only the slogans stay to say
the context of the vanished act of faith.

>   Cities are not so different in the dark.
>   They all have places where
>   the face has mouldered to expose the bone,
>   where slogans terrorize and drops of blood
>   appear and disappear. Stigmata of despair.

Fred Brown

PEACE IS HERE

If you could foretell the mind of
divided people then a genius you would be.
Of years of strife and trouble
with grief and tragedy.
Could the road of time be circled
with a peace that will remain
and heal the wounds of sadness
where people they were slain.

A smile on someone's face
It doesn't say that they are glad
Behind that smile sadness lurks
of the sorrows that they had.
Now a roadway there where peace prevails
A voice as one resound
Calling to all people just to rally round.

To show that way when others fail
And not to carry from the past.
A vegenvies of great hatred
Look peace is here at last.

John Monaghan

THE TEARS OF THE ISLE

Many, many tears have flowed
On this beautiful Emerald Isle
But no-one seems to take the time
To stop and think awhile.

Think of the parents grieving
O'er the death of their 6 year old son
Playing football in the street
He was killed by a sniper's gun.

Think of the tears of a sweetheart
When she hears that her soldier boy
Lies silent in the mortuary
Shot dead by the gunman's toy.

Think of the widow mourning
The loss of a loving spouse
He was a 'legitimate target'
For building a policeman's house.

Think of the tears of the children
They cannot understand
Why a bomb sent their daddy
So soon, to the Promised Land.

If the gunmen would lay down their arms
And think of the sorrow meanwhile
Maybe their hearts would be softened
By the tears of the Emerald Isle.

Margaret Tate

FALSE HOPE

The headlines read 'It's over',
But we are not so sure,
Is this another tactic,
Another means to lure
Us into false security,
To break the barriers down,
A means to get what they think
Is theirs by right to own?
The troops are moving out now,
But this just brings to mind
Echoes of their old demands,
'Troops out' out of our land.
They've got their first concession,
But still they demand more,
'Open up cross border roads
To the state they were before.'
The Irish and Americans
Think the solution will be theirs,
If only they would learn to keep
Out of British affairs.
They get still more concessions,
But what have they to give?
They could yield up their weapons
And let their country's men live.
But no! Negotiations
Is all they have in mind,
And they are not prepared to wait
'Til a settlement is signed.
So for our children's children
A solution we must find.

Colin Ross

NO MORE

No more dirty dangerous mines,
No more work or jobs for life,
No more basic fuel from land,
No more coal - their time is done.
No more shifts through day or night,
No more for young and old alike,
No more pits for man or machines,
No more mines - they're history.
No more damp, cold gasses in our chest,
No more carefully watching our steps.
No more accidents close to death,
No more tales our kids to tell.
No more excitement or thrill in life,
No more hope here for young lives.
No more spending power of mine,
No more dining out with wine.
No more folk visit our village so dear,
No more carnivals, street parties or fairs.
No more drinks in miners' clubs,
No more fun and laughs for us.
No more sports cars to show off,
No more girls come here to chat.
No more shops doing a 'jolly good run',
No more holidays where there's sun.
No more 'feel good factor' in the air,
No more prosperity, only a despair.
No more fresh thoughts come to mind . . .
Only a sadness growing with time.

D Gupta

THOUGHTS

The governments hold on to the White Paper
      Anything else is on computer data
      No jobs are left no weekly pay
Our men stay at home with nothing to do all day.
      One time you could go to someone's door
      'Just for a chat' but not anymore

People would smile or call to see you were OK
      That doesn't happen, not today
Kids used to play outside their door
      But that's not safe, not anymore

Once we had laughter a smile or a grin
      Even that seems to be a sin
      No houses no money nothing left
The years have gone by, the times you want to forget

V Robson

DISAPPOINTMENT

Whole day
Search for job,
Brought him
Disappointment
And dismay.

The hungry stomach
And tired legs,
Made him
Totally nay.

His Degree
Laughed at him,
As his fate
Gone away.

His hopes
And expectations too,
Turned into
Useless hay.

Once again
In search of hope,
He kneeled and made
A humble pray.

Suddenly when
He realised
The soaring unemployment,
He gave up
The hope of ray.

Dr Ranjit Kanwar

THE TRAMP OF ARGO

He sat alone the Tramp of Argo
Amusingly joked about,
Made the one man show.
Dirty and smelly with whiskers
turned grey, 'turn him out',
I heard them say.
With baggy top coat and small
peaked cap, my feeling was of pity
for that poor old chap.
His belongings by his side
In holed carrier bag, and
between his chapped lips, was
the remains of a well smoked fag.
He sat almost unmoving, while
jokes of scorn were stressed thick
and fast,
And as I glanced at the Tramp of Argo,
I thought, 'poor thing' he can't have
long to last.
Seemingly unmoved by tasteless words
said,
I gathered the Tramp of Argo wished
he was dead.

Kenneth Storey

MISTY MORNING IN THE FENS

The misty, ancient army stands still in the age-old fen
Two horizontal rows with bushy clothes
Visible afar, a row of slender, upright men
Silent and ready - endless warriors froze -
Soldiers? Once time, but now revealed in the hazy breeze
They're not the proud militia - only rows of trees.

And, look to the other side where my dogs play -
Shapes quietly looming out of the wispy day.
Echoing across the bank a long-drawn ghostly cry.
Bugles of ancient Angles? No, the low and mournful sigh
Of mothers calling for their sons, just newly snatched away
Crated up and sent abroad and fattened for the day
When human gluttons ooze the taste, with eyes a-greed with zeal
Slobb'ring over little creatures - lean and tasty veal.

Yet their mothers do not fear nor hate the human race
Patience, tolerance and pity sit on the bovine face.
Dear cows, you gaze with sorrow, down on my dogs and me
Please forgive our wicked wantonness, our greed and cruelty.

Penny Scales

UNTIL THE PILL

When we've reached the magic number and things are breaking down
and we're pretty sure there's not much left to do,
we're going to the bridge that spans the river
the residents of Blossom Avenue.

In a show of solidarity against the going rule,
the one that says you have to stick around,
we're going to do the only thing that's left us
until a better answer can be found.

Not for us the sorrow of slow parting,
rotting limbs and brand new bedsores every day,
having visits from your dearest banging on about the weather
when it's clear you've all got nothing left to say.

The magic pill's not here yet, at least it's not allowed so
the lot of us know what we're going to do.
We're holding hands and jumping in the river,
the residents of Blossom Avenue.

Megan Walden

SELF KNOWLEDGE

I've been told
It has been said
That I should invest in myself.
Since I do not have a tower of confidence
      Building up inside.
I've begun to gain some self knowledge
      About myself.
      And I find it scary
Hearing things said about me
      Not in my presence
      To my face and behind my back
      Some good and some bad.
Throughout it all - I'm surviving somehow.
What do I need to know about myself?
Because I don't know who I am
What aspirations, expectations or even goals I have.
      My mind is confused
      My time is now
          The end is near.

Zubair Ahmed Mirza

DEAD OR ALIVE?

The doctor said, 'He's still alive.'
He lies upon the bed
With vacant eyes he stares about,
I know his soul is dead.

In hospital in shuffling line,
Slithering, slippered feet,
The shells of men are led,
Although their hearts still beat.

My father looks the same,
But the stroke which took his mind
Has taken him away from me,
Leaving a void behind.

Three years he breathed and ate,
A man already dead,
With only whirling, misty thoughts
Thronging his handsome head.

P R Mason

SHOULD I SAY ANYTHING . . .

the pain she bore - the thoughts she thought
the warmth she gave - her love, her strength
her warmth again - she shared it all
it was all she ever knew (it was her choice?)

a tear fell and her feelings spilled - they were so strong -
overwhelming - overpowering - everything was still
their anxiousness was aloud - their fear was felt
their presence created an atmosphere of confusion - disillusion

she wasn't that tall - like they had thought
she was a tower - was one in the forefront
they were wrong - they were

a tear fell and her feelings spilled
so did they - they fell - they were lost -
they were encompassed in an illusion -
they had created - it was all their fault

sad - is it not?

Jacqueline Miller

FROM HOME TO HOME

I thought you must be dead, he wrote,
Then saw your name
Congratulated on your ninety years
In a parish magazine.

I am, she wrote to him,
In all but ticking heart
And just a little brain.
Can't move, alas! I thought, of course
That you had gone and envied you.
You write, though, from a nursing home.
Poor you, then, too.

Griselda Scott

ONE OF LIFE'S LITTLE PROBLEMS

There is many a good ride on a horse's hide
Many a good ride on a pony,
But the struggle and strife as we go through life
Can be yours if you ride on your own'y

There seems little sense jumping over a fence
If not sure what's on the other side.
You could be a bimbo and try the limbo
But that too could damage your pride.

So, if under or over you may not be in clover
Take the reins, use your brains in a fix
Study the books and with your good looks
You will knock all the fences for six.

Cliff Wilson

63

THE SLEEPING DEATH

I lay in my bed
Tied to machines
One gives me blood
And one makes me breathe
My thoughts in my head
That no-one can hear
I'm lost in the darkness
The pain and the fear

My thoughts are now twisted
This lifeline of pills
This pain in my body
I pray you will kill
Someone switch off
This machine giving life
Let me leave this pain
And run to the light

My time is up gladly
But you keep me here
In pain I'm existing
The darkness and fear
You cannot hear me
But you know what's best?
I pray to the Lord
Now lay me to rest

Lee Robinson

PHILIPPINO ANGELS

Children for sale
Sad eyes that see
No future and no joy.
No chance to play.
A toy for tawdry hands -
Expecting pain and tears.
The years ahead
Stretch hopeless.
Such perfect bodies
Not yet fully formed.
Their innocence betrayed.
Can we be uninvolved?
We read, we watch TV.
We know, we witness -
We do nothing!

June E Morgan

SHOW MERCY

Do you see me sitting here,
And if so, do you really care?
I cannot talk, can hardly see
Yet once so hardy, strong and free.
I rage within, my body screams
The anger of fire that burns the whin,
The fury of soldiers going into battle,
The roar of the lion, the snake to rattle.
The thundering sound of the water calls
As it cuts through the rocks and heads for the falls,
The canoeists adrenaline pumping so fast,
The resolve of the runner not to be last.
I sit here rocking from side to side
Trying to talk but the words seem to hide,
You smile and pat my head as you leave,
Please honour our pact and have me freed.

Jacqueline D Rhodes

I CRIED

Skeleton face, hair falling out, dressed
        Like a duchess, I wanted to shout
           'Let my mother die!'

Earrings and bangles, baubles and rings
Like a clown in the circus, with
        Lipstick and things
           Her dignity was gone.

Only her eyes and the shake of her head
Told me:-
        'I know you wish me dead to ease my
           Suffering - don't!'

           I cried!

Kate Brown

THE ROAD TO GOD KNOWS WHERE

Take my hand
Let's run away
Leave this town
It's cold and grey
Find new life
I'm sick and tired
There must be more
On the other side

Leave your clothes
Cut your hair
Take the road
To God knows where
Burn your house
Steal a car
Don't look back
We've come this far

Miles and miles
Of burning sand
I see you smile
I think you understand
I see the end
It's drawing near
Close your eyes
Nothing to fear
Feel the pain
Give up your soul
Free as the birds
We've lost control

Jake Baker

THE LAST RITES

Before I decided to take your life -
There were so many questions to be answered.
But where could I go for help?
Who would have given me advice?
Yes you were right:
Just no-one at all.

I had to taste the wine
At the bedside.
It was supposed to be
The last party I gave you
But you were too weak to drink it.

Gone are the days of caring
And sharing the sorrows and happiness
Of everyone's life.
Everybody is looking -
But nobody is watching.

All I have of you are letters;
A thousand photographs
Framed in silver and gold
And the rich cologne you wore.

Doctors said you had to go into hospital;
But I knew better - and you knew that too.
Sharing your life was full of joy -
So sharing your death was nothing
That I wanted to destroy.

One day I shall tell your children -
The fate I gave you
And what I had to face.
I hope for forgiveness from the one and only
For He should know
Where you had to go.

Jagdeesh Sokhal

SEGREGATION ON THE PAGE

Boxes on application forms
 - British European,
Asian, Chinese, Indian,
Afro-Caribbean
 - segregation on the page
and all around the world,
with rage and anger rampant
as racist taunts are hurled.

We pride ourselves on feats
in science and technology
yet we still can't manage
to live in harmony.
Customs and beliefs
may vary far and wide,
tainted by segregation,
war and apartheid.

Will the next generation
bring lasting peace
and succeed in seeing
racism cease?

Julie A Kinnair

FIXING VIEWS

Sometimes I doubt myself when
I say I am not racist,
Maybe I should say I wish I
Was not.

My father is, did I learn it?
I wish I had not. But I
Will try to change. I will
Endeavour

To correct this fault of mine.
I hope one day to stand
Up and be counted fully,
Against this

Negative discrimination. Then
I can say smiling, with a
Confident gesture, that I am
Not racist.

Tracey Brown

RULES OF THE EMPLOYER

One man is clever,
Was top of his class,
Can do the job well,
Can do it quite fast.

The other is thick,
Didn't pass his exam,
Doesn't know what to do,
His brain is a sham.

The choice seems obvious,
The decision looks clear,
But what you might think,
Doesn't happen here.

The dumb man wins,
The smart man's 'not right',
For one man is black,
And the other one white.

Sarah Bennett

WHY?

So, you like the music, yeah?
So, you like the beat.
So, you like the rhythm, yeah?
So, why don't you like us?

You like our dreadlocked hair, yeah?
You copycat our style.
You really try to be like us, don't you, yeah?
You don't like us - why?

Is it envy that you feel of us?
Is it fear of what you do not understand?
Is it the darker shade of pale?
Is this why you don't like us?

Don't you know that we might envy you?
Don't you know how much you may scare us?
Don't you think we might like to be you?
Don't you think we like you?

Why?

Mary Brooke

ME RACIST?

Racism! Huh, I'm not racist
These poor people are just a victim of circumstance
Been born into it or brainwashed
No other way to go
No I've got nothing against them
Think everyone should have one
Some are quite clever you know!
And you've just got to give them a chance
Anyway I wouldn't see one out on the streets
Perhaps even take him home
They're OK, quite harmless really
Don't know why people can't leave them alone
No I'm not racist.

C Carlin

ETHNIC CLEANSING?

Pharaoh enslaved the Israelites
Joshua slaughtered the Canaanites
Saul destroyed the Amenkalites
Sadem tried to take the Kuwaitis

Mladic ethnic cleansed the Bosnians' rights
In these days of so many human plights.
Unlearned lessons of years of hindsights
Led us to believe the Pharisees and Hypocrites

Did their most sacred and holy Mights
Really guide them to *blow-away* those humans' rights?

Or, are they, like their gods, colossal deceits:
The contrivances of mankind's atrocious fetes

Is there, yet, a glimmer of hope for humanity
To shed those self-righteous deeds of sanctity?
To learn of love and real equality
And, preserve life, even unto this day!

William Peters

THE STATE I AM IN

There's really not much the matter with me
Although I am not as fit as I'd like to be.
I have arthritis, in neck, hips, and knees
Bronchitis makes me talk with a wheeze
My pulse is erratic, my blood is thin.
But 'I am awfully well for the state I am in.'

Arch supports I have for my feet.
Without them I wouldn't be out on the street.
Sleep is denied me night after night.
Yet still every morning I find I am alright
My memory's failing my head's in a spin
But 'I am awfully well for the state I am in.'

Old age is golden, I've oft heard it said.
But sometimes I wonder as I crawl into bed
My specs in their scabbard, my teeth in a cup
Hernia truss at my bed, for when I get up
Ere sleep overtakes me I think to myself.
Is there anything else to put on the shelf.
I've stopped drinking whisky, and I don't sip the gin.
But 'I am awfully well for the state I am in.'

How do I know my youth is all spent
Well my get up and go, has got up and went
I really don't mind, as I think with a grin.
Of all the grand places my get up has been.
I rise up each morning, I dust down my wits.
I pick up the papers and read the obits.
If my name isn't in them I know I am not dead
So I have a good breakfast and go back to bed
I lie for a while praise God with a hymn
Cause 'I am awfully well for the state I am in.'

W McKirdy

UNNECESSARY GREED

The hedge is part of the country way of life
The fruits it provides are scrumptious and rife

The hedge has been with us since the dawn of time
It also protects the wildlife and keeps it in its prime

The farmer ripped out the hedge and planted more seed
Reaping and extra yield from the field

But how much benefit did the land yield
Compared to the hedge that once stretched across the field

How can it be measured against the song of a bird
As it sings from a bramble to a splash of willowherb

And when the day has past and there is no light
When no nightingale sings through the night

When gone is the hedge that once was their home
Along with the wild flowers and the mountain rowan

How can you compare it with man and his greed
When the things he doesn't require becomes a weed

Wild flowers insects butterflies will never return
Along with the partridge that once nested in the fern

John Anderton

WORKING FROM HOME

In and out in less than a second,
Moving faster and faster towards the end,
Slipping and sliding
In and out riding,
Eyes closed, breathing fast,
How long is this going to last?

He lunges hard eyes rolling back,
Panting as he empties his sack,
Pulling away after a few moments' pleasure,
All I can think about is the weather!

Clean and dressed he stands at the door,
Fifty quid in my hand and arranging for more.
'Same time next week. See you then.'
Slamming the door on his back again.

Why do I feel as if I'm dirty?
Why do I do this still?
Rent's paid, TV too,
Why is it this I do?
Money for a few moments' pleasure,
All this so that I don't lose Heather.

Mandy Ward

IN MEMORY OF JIAN XUN AGED 10 YEARS

Jian Xun lies dead
starved
tethered
to his stinking welfare-bed.

No-one mourns his passing,
cold, painful
and so slow . . .
Juidi Jiejue
child-killing
by decree.

An hour after dying
Jian's feeble wrists
untied,
his body's swift cremation
all existence
now denied.

We read it here
in black and white
China's children,
chosen . . .
to die.

Sue Hansard

ODE TO THE LOTTERY BOSSES

Charity begins at home
Often said but true
The people need a lot of things
Here are just a few

We don't care about the millennium
Just about what it will cost
We think about the cut backs
And the lives that will be lost

We want to make our children safe
From the lunatics that are around
We want shelters for the homeless
We want cures to be found

It sometimes takes a tragedy
To make the people see
But we don't want art and opera
From the national lottery

We want to help the blind to see
And help the deaf to hear
We want services for the elderly
Security for those who live in fear

Sport and leisure centres
We can live without
There are more deserving causes
Why not make the money count

Let's raise a glass to Camelot
They may have money to spend
But they've no idea of priorities
It's the people who pay in the end

Fiona McPhee

ON VIVISECTION

This is a plea for those that are silent
And suffering tortures dealt by man,
The animals kept caged, unloved in laboratories
Taking part in some scientific plan.

The rabbit, its body permanently twisted
The cat with stitches across it's head,
The rats and guinea-pigs partially paralysed
I see them and how I wish they were dead.

Faithful dogs that only live to please
Subdued, confused, eyes smarting with pain,
Clever man, tell me, why so sadistic
Is this human progress, no it's insane.

What price the lipstick, shampoo or detergent
Or how much tobacco will cause cancer,
These animals know of the time and expense
For in their suffering lies the answer.

We who have our pets and love them
See you as perverse, yes and obscene,
Master torturers of innocent creatures
We wonder, do you really sleep serene.

But you say, all this is necessary
To find cures for the diseases of mankind,
And you dare say, that these lesser animals
Well, just do not possess a reasoning mind.

Jo Rosson Gaskin

LAND OF OPPORTUNITY

In this land of opportunity,
Make money without hitch.
In this free community,
We do not tax the rich.

They must have an incentive,
To make more and more and more.
But no matter how inventive,
The poor must still stay poor.

'Pay peanuts, get monkeys' they say -
These monkeys who've had it so tough.
So when they want to double their pay,
How is it *they're* good enough?

Why did they take these peanut jobs
For a thousand pounds a day?
They must have been aimed at low quality yobs
Who'd accept such measly pay!

But as for the poor,
That's different.
They can't be worth more,
They're so idle and insolent.

They must learn responsibility.
They cannot have immunity
From this tax and VAT without pity
In this land of opportunity.

Derek Metson

ROOT OF ALL EVIL

The nights are drawing in
And outside is cold and wet
But even a warm bed
Will not stop me worry about debt

As I lie here alone in bed
Watch the hours ticking by
As my problems take over
I just sit alone and cry

Will I ever get some money
To get back on my feet
I feel things will never change
Looking at the bills on the seat

Staring at them lying there
Is breaking my aching heart
Why can't I have enough money
To live and make a fresh start

Money is the root of all evil
Well that is what people say
But if I could just get enough
Then all my bills I would pay

But what is the use of dreaming
Of a day that will not come
I feel I'm losing everything
And it's left me really numb.

J Everson

WHY US?

Everybody laughing,
Everybody sneering,
Kick you in the gutter,
'Cause they just don't care.

Street life,
Such strife,
Why me?

Lying on benches,
Covered in yesterday's news,
Begging at the bakery,
For stale bread and cakes.

Street life,
Such strife,
Why me?

Meeting other people in my situation,
Hearing their tales of what's happened to them,
Realising I'm not worse off,
Feeling bad for them.

Street life,
Such strife,
Why us?

Lauren Ketchell

CHANGING TIMES

Times are changing from bad to worse
You venture out someone steals your purse
You go to sleep without a care in the world
Only to be awoken there's an intruder downstairs.
Where are the people that we once knew?
Who would tip their hats and say 'How do you do'
These times have gone they'll never come back
Why is the world looking gloomy and black.

There's no such thing as a walk in the park
You fear the daytime never mind the dark
The violence is growing you can't walk the street
You're always in fear of whom you might meet
An innocent trip to the shop for some sugar
Turn your back the victim of a mugger
The day will come when it won't be so grim
We can rid these undesirables into the bin.

Now we can look forward to a safer new life
Not worrying about anyone brandishing a knife
The streets will be safer as you grow older
You won't have to keep on looking over your shoulder
So that is how the world should be
A better life for you and me.

Mary Kirby

A BOOM TO BOOST TORY ELECTION HOPES

Our Health Service is flagging,
Education is lagging,
Redundancy you may expect.
But the headlines do say
There's a boom on the way,
The economy not under threat.

Our assets have been stripped,
And our savings have dipped,
Our security may disappear.
We may lose our home,
So the streets have to roam,
But, we have nothing to fear.

Oh! What a surprise,
Yet another rise
Is on the cards for the MP's.
I thought the intention,
Was to raise the pension
For all the over sixties.

Postal workers on strike,
Because they have the ike,
With conditions they are dissatisfied.
But, in spite of our plight,
We are doing alright,
For we still have our great *British pride.*

Eileen A Morris

OUT OF AFRICA

Dark eyes,
Dark skin,
A hungry child hanging
From a limp and empty breast.

Scorched earth,
Failed crop,
A grieving mother sobbing
As her child is laid to rest . . .

On the dust routes of the continent
The fighting factions seize the foreign grain,
Feeding troops, fuelling war,
Glasnost guns on African terrain.

While people sweat in shanty towns
The generals plot in air conditioned rooms,
And children starve on fruitless plains,
Through drought and war the spreading desert looms.

Diamonds, gold and minerals,
A diverse land of riches unsurpassed,
Yet still the children plead for life,
To quench their thirst, to end their helpless fast . . .

Dark eyes,
Dark skin,
The beauty of a child
On a full and healthy breast.

Soaked earth,
Harvest reaped,
The promise of a future
And their sorrow put to rest.

Kit Moreton

NO FIXED ABODE

We are the non persons who come to your town,
Hate, like or loathe us, you smile, with a frown.
As our homes all pull up,
And you see us around.
No fixed abode,
No rights to the road
They say we're a culture,
And yet one with no future . . .
You probably haven't met us,
Try to live how we do,
And be who we are,
As we don't have a mortgage, or a company car -
We live on the line,
And travel too far.
Our families alive -
It struggles survives
It is your insecurity
That threatens your purity -
Not ours.

Cal Buffery

DOWN AND OUT

The old tramp sits on his own
He's got nowhere to call his home
Down and out, not always so
Now he's got no place to go

Fate has dealt him, a cruel blow
Sits here rocking to and fro
Looks back, on days when he could sing
Back on days, when he was king

Shuffles to the underpass
Knows his health is fading fast
Cardboard box here for his bed
World is spinning in his head

Old man found in state of decay
That is all the papers say
One less soul for us to save
Lay him in a paupers grave

No-one cried for this old man
No-one knew him, no-one can
Now he lays beneath the earth
Covered by the green green turf

No marker here to give his name
At his passing, no-one came
No more cold streets for him to roam
Now at last he's found his home.

Dave Hesmer

CARDBOARD CITY

When passing me by save your pity for someone else
You do not know the circumstances you see
Not too long ago I lived a life of luxury
It soon got boring and was not for me.

I joined the homeless in the cardboard city
Another stranger on the street with carrier bags
Away from the rat race, free as a bird soaring high
Sleeping rough, with worn out shoes, and clothes in rags.

Seeing wino's drink methylated spirits, getting high
The charity van, bringing sandwiches and tea
Everyone looking gaunt and hungry
Eager for food and drink including me.

Life was hard on the street all huddled together
Here were true friends, that are hard to find
Having survived now in these two different worlds
Which do I choose rich or poor, one must be left behind.

Picking up the carrier bags, I make my way to the train
That will take me back to the life I had forsaken
My friends have no choice, they are not as fortunate as me
There is only the rough, lonely road they have taken.

Brenda Colvin

GRAMMAR SCHOOLS

It was in 1970 grammar schools were closed
Margaret Thatcher did it though opposed

She said she had a clear vision of education
although it was a policy of eradication

The advantages were bandied about
and all opposition thrown out

There was nothing one could do
The lady told us what to do

Education policy became a political football
and the future of our children was not the goal

Worried parents had no choice
no-one heard their voice

Politicians made the final decision
It was now obsession

Soon the people gave up
they were simply fed up

The rich have private schools for their darlings
the poor had no chance for their siblings

Everyone would have lived happily after
if things did not start to alter

Now grammar schools are to be doubled
at a cost of billions the government is not troubled

But they are cutting 17 million from university funds
creating a job loss of 3000 university dons

So do we have an education policy
or is it just odyssey?

I doubt politicians will tell us
and are going to simply mess us

Parents are going to be left with anxiety
ending up as a mixed up society

Albert Moses

TEARS

I say a prayer
as the tears fall
that all the persecuted
will stand tall
That they'll find it in their hearts
to forgive the wrong
and the narrow-mindedness
that's gone on for so long
Living, breathing, talking together,
standing shoulder to shoulder
You'd think our attitudes would change
as we all get older.
Yet still there are those blinded to the truth
as racism rears its ugly head
all the prejudice and discrimination
the bigotry and hatred
It's lingering there . . .
ready to pounce.
Waiting to strike us -
and pull us all down.

Natasha Cobbold

EUTHANASIA

I've been sitting here in this chair,
with my body not moving and the same kind of stare.
I've been like this for five years or more,
with a blank expression, just staring at the wall.
I cannot move my arms or legs, being drip fed,
and talking to you from inside my head.
I'm an old man now and tired of this wasteful life,
just inject me and let me die.

Euthanasia is the key, the key for my soul to be set free.
So I can talk and walk and run again,
let me out of this cell, locked away in pain.
A simple injection, ten seconds I'm gone,
away from this world and into the next one.

C Leith

WHY?

I sometimes sit and wonder,
Why the world's in such a mess,
Why the governments around the world,
With peoples' lives, play chess.

Why some make war for power,
And some make war for greed,
And some make war, not caring,
What's a person's race or creed.

Why some can live in harmony,
If black or brown or white,
And some folk find the slightest thing,
To go to war and fight.

Why old folk get so frightened,
Just walking down the street,
Afraid to pass the time of day,
So scared of who they'll meet.

Why some folk always argue,
They shouldn't really care,
About what Mr Jones has got,
There's plenty round to share.

Some people worry too much,
'Till they can't cope no more,
Some people find it hard to live,
No matter rich or poor.

I'd like to think there's someone,
Who looks down from above,
In heaven; life hereafter,
A world that's filled with love.

F W Cumbes

RESPECT

The word just will not do.
It must encompass more that that
To get the message thro',
Thro' to all the people
Who sometimes do not care
What happens to the animals
Whose lives they do not share.
We must give more than just respect
It's love and caring too
So that in tine the whole wide world
Will think just as we do.

D Meyer

ON THE DOVE AT SANTA MARIA DEGLI ANGELI

Are you real,
Little white dove sitting motionless
In your nest upheld in Francis' hands
At the end of a glass-covered corridor?

Or are you a pot or plastic simulacrum,
Part of a plot to portray the bird-loving saint
Of sentimental hagiography?

I stand and watch for any movement.
But your head remains fixed in one direction,
Not a feather stirs, eyes without motion stare.

I move away and look at other things.

But the question gnaws at my mind: are you real?
I return to look again and you are still there.
But now you've turned and face the other way,
Still motionless.

So you are real. But why do you stay unmoved?
What love draws you to that plaster nest
And holds you bound there?
Don't you ever fly away? But where would you go?
Sky and grass mock through solid glass
Unattainable.

There's water in the trough at the saint's feet,
And doubtless they put food in the upheld nest.
But what roots you there and keeps you motionless?

Is it the love the living Francis felt
For every single creature of God's fashioning
That the birds gathered and listened to his preaching?
Is it the pure abandon of his self-giving to God?

Or are you merely keeping the saint company
In his lonely ecstasy at the end of the corridor?

Derek Rawcliffe

THE HUMAN DISGRACE

In the name of science we kill and maim.
And just for sport we shoot at game,
To entertain we whip and train,
These things, we are doing now.
Are animals just ours to use,
To love or hate or just abuse,
We do these things just to amuse,
Can someone tell me how,
Yes how, can we still act so cruel,
Some might just say that I'm being a fool,
This planet it is ours to rule.
So let us take a bow.
You see to me, this all seems wrong,
To the human race we all belong,
We say compassion is still strong,
Yet the hunter mops his brow,
As the hounds they tear a fox apart,
And humans laugh as they howl and bark,
Do these people have a heart,
I think not, somehow.
But me, I have a dream at night,
I see a scientist under a rabbit's knife,
Then a fox with a gun take a hunter's life,
A human steak cooked by a cow.

R M Pengelly

HAROLD 'LORD' WILSON IS DEAD

An essay I wrote yesterday
Praised your achievements to the skies.
My mother never liked your voice
And your son was called Giles -
Were you ever a *working-class hero?*

Tony Blair scarcely remembers your first governments.
Ted Heath's obituary was so sincere.
In death you unite everyone,
Even your wife and mistress.
The red flag shall fly half-mast for you.

John Smith died a year ago.
He didn't win four elections
Or establish the Open University.
Why did your Gannex Mac and pipe
Inspire so many bleeding hearts?

If children in the comprehensives you created
Fail to recognise Winston Churchill
Then what epitaph could be so great
That they will remember you?

All the Tory tabloids have written obituaries
And four-page pullouts about your life.
'Do you remember the sixties?' is a PR reteo exercise.
When Baroness Thatcher dies
We will have a period of national mourning.

Nick Brunel

CARELESS CREATURE

There's a creature, who walks our earth
Who is more powerful, than the forces of nature.
Whether for financial gain or a scientific venture
He'll ruin this planet, for all he is worth.

His careless nature, fills our oceans with oil
Suffocating marine life, when oil and water collide.
It's polluting our once picturesque rocky shores
As it rolls in, with the coming of each tide.

Our ozone layer, is being eaten away so steadily
As new-age chemicals are emitted into our skies.
Causing our earth's temperature to slowly rise,
Thus creating this unnatural global warming.

Tropical rainforests, so full of colour and life
Are rapidly being chopped down, without a care.
Beautiful and exotic plants no longer thrive.
Evicted animals, their homes are no longer there.

This planet, our home, is a beautiful place
Yet, it's being killed off at an alarming pace.
If this creature doesn't change his ways
Soon there'll be no Earth worth walking on.
With no respect, all is lost, all is gone.

Stephanie Bones

IN VAIN PURSUIT

On seeing fur coats displayed in a shop
Think for a moment, it's time to stop
The killing of animals for vanity sake
Innocent creatures, whose lives that we take

To satisfy human status, is just a fact
Displaying our wealth by destroying wild cats
Ocelots, fox, seal and lynx
Creatures, cruel traps and farming minks

Velvets and satins, lace designer wear
Respecting the animals, shows that we care
Fashion designers, with many fabric choices
Animals' rights, have only their voices
To speak up for God's creatures, who can't speak for themselves.

Rita Humphrey

FOX HUNTING

See the fox jump
See the fox run
See the fox
Play with his young

See the big red hunter
Polish up his gun
See the big hunter
Kill the fox for fun

J C Walters

OUR NEW WORLD WITH AN OPEN MIND

Open your eyes and look around,
You see the world without its stand,
Pulled from all over to its destruction,
It cries so loudly for helping action,
Too many people, too many cars,
Fumes mark the world with ugly scars,
Industrial leaks, pollution, waste,
It all gave the world a disfigured face,
Once simple, pure and beautiful,
Unspoiled, unused, happy and full,
Then man came and ruined its look,
He opened the chapter, of World Decay Book,
And from that moment till recent times,
There was so many, world abuse crimes,
And every country has had its share,
No matter when, which one or where,
Europe, Africa, the States and East,
It doesn't even complete the list,
The rich ones, the poor ones,
They all gave world the look that counts,
They haven't been sentenced and jailed for life,
How come! All of them have handled the destructive knife,
Who is to judge them? The same people are!
So wake up now and make a new start.

Anna Bayless

PAY OUT SHARES!

Deep down men must work
To line the pockets of the government's urge
To sweep the slate clean,
The waste of hell;
Each man must die so what the hell.
Rebirth is strong in plastic tubes
Yet food is scarce:
Only those who work will eat the dirt;
Out of the cans that's full of preserve.
Peas are green the grass grows brown
The cattle feed a government's girth;
Fattening up rosy cheeks
While the people starve who're out of work.
Cut off gas, the electric light
Water that's stale from polluted earth.
Pay your bills to pay out shares
Or freeze to death in modern times,
Because the government says it cares.
Children of the world take care,
Computers say your turn will come
To push the button to end the war;
Because the governments of the world:-
Really do care for you.
So eat your food and pay your bills
Work the earth or dig the holes,
A new silo needs to be filled,
It's all to protect you out there. . .

Alan Bowman

THE EYES HAVE IT

Now Mr Blair
You really stare
With those demonic eyes
From Tory poster lies

It is unfair
I do declare
To show you in this guise
But really no surprise

Peeping through the curtain
Your critics may be certain
Friends may find it scary
Others think it hairy

Do not despair
Or tear your hair
May be sinister
But next year Prime Minister

M Barnett

PARTY POLITICS

Party politics are headline news
MP's and councillors air their views
How often do they change after an election
Stubbing out the electorate's objections
If it's breaking the law to publicly lie
How are they always able to defy
To say one thing and then deny
To be elected for a cause
And then hide behind party rules
Preaching one thing and doing another
While looking after one's brother
We elect parties to be our voice
Often things they do are not our choice
So potential politicians take heed
It's us the electorate that you need

D Allen

INFORMATION

We hope you have enjoyed reading this book - and that you will continue to enjoy it in the coming years.

If you like reading and writing poetry drop us a line, or give us a call, and we'll send you a free information pack.

Write to

Anchor Books Information
1-2 Wainman Road
Woodston
Peterborough
PE2 7BU